Edward Barrett
Common Preludes

Edward Barrett
Common Preludes

The Groundwater Press
Hudson, New York

Cover photograph by Ben E. Watkins.

Acknowledgments

My thanks to the editors of the following journals where these poems were published: *Partisan Review*, "The True Story"; *o-blek*, "Tripoline," "Theory of Transportation," "Sonnet," "Essays for the Moment"; *Agni*, "Odeon," "Vermont House"; *lift*, "Viking Melody," "Derivation of Equations," "Canvas," "Nine Acts That Would Have Killed Vaudeville"; *Painted Bride Quarterly*, "Stage Directions"; *Mothers of Mud*, "The Ocean People Live Near the Ocean," "Morfudd's Hair"; *Newark Review*, "Toward Blue Peninsula," "Live Acts"; *Brooklyn Review*, "Still Life with Roadmap"; *lingo*, "The Leaves Are Something This Year."

"Second Letter to Jack Spicer" was published in *That Various Field* (Figures Press, Great Barrington, MA). "Looking for Halley's Comet with Liz" was published in *Fire Readings* (Frank Books, Vincennes, France). "Secret Tapes," and "Fragment of a Haiku" were published in *7x3* (Kendall Gallery, NYC). My thanks to the editors of these anthologies.

Portions of the poem "Common Preludes" were published in a multimedia collection, *Shoebox* (Paris, France).

"Theory of Transportation," "The Hat," "Somebody's Terrace on Ninth Avenue," "Dunquin," "Powder River," "Haying," "Screenbolical," "Lisa, Your Beautiful Friend Is Here," "Secret Tapes" were published in a limited edition chapbook, *Theory of Transportation*, Groundwater Press, 1990.

I am grateful to the Fund for Poetry for a grant.

The Groundwater Press
Post Office Box 704
Hudson, New York 12534

ISBN 0-922792-67-4

CONTENTS

Sonnet

1.

The graffiti should read *sweep my hair back gently, leaving the cornice its question of light.* If you understand anything about the way we live now, you know how the plot thinned out, the orange peel slides off in one of those perfect citrus spirals, our stare more serious than we let on. Columns of traffic in midtown wait like an intentional misgiving whose tears are iron in place of the god unaccustomed to grief. His children don't live forever and for this he blames them, for this he fashions riddles and labyrinths to keep them occupied until the mouse gnawing at the baseboard triggers a secret spring and the wall flies open and the shield and a tank-top (a little tight, a little skimpy) are revealed.

2.

Summer accumulated in a series of private lines and bee-stings, flesh reddening and peeling like a clock. Constant repair taught the blue and white harbor how pure an event thought was. Perfection was there, disguised as imperfection. Loss was disguised as abundance, to which there was no answering except normally, as if sheer presence sent a shock you could afterwards appoint notes to, neither aggrieved nor congruent, but another surface which threw you into history simply because you replied.

3.

The green swirl of light, off-center behind a ridge of pines not
immersed in darkness but somehow giving that off like a hollow
sun. My head is not seen, just as the pines really are there, just
not visible in the wedge-shaped dark that intersects the distance
to make this the foreground—"this" being where we stand (you
are not seen too, so this isn't a self-portrait by any means)—
neither one of us looking at the swirling light or the pines and
the dark rising out of them: "this" not a self-documenting uni-
verse but an applied chance that tugs at the longstanding yet
abrupt sense that it would continue when you weren't there—
would continue *because* you weren't there, marking by cadence
the having it at all.

4.

That ham and cheese sandwich was delicious. A moment ago I
was worrying about something (how we live now is to worry
about something, usually one big thing) until I wasn't worrying
about it and instead was thinking about you and the funny half-
light I see when I look at you. Part of this island has death
written over it a thousand times, part lime juice and salt, part a
custom-made sailor's jacket with gold piping across the breast—
an essay in the form of a blazer—so that when you turn your
head to the side like that, this is holding you here.

Second Letter to Jack Spicer

for James Schuyler

Last night I was out with two friends I love very much although
I'm not in love with either of them. It's a relief to have friends
you love but don't fall in love with although you can never be
sure that won't happen, or if it doesn't happen is it because of
something you're not looking at, something unformed? Who said
we don't have souls when we're born but make them up as we go
along? I don't really believe this since so many things seem
hardwired-in from the start, but I like the idea because it makes
me think the point of something is that it be fully realized and
that you get to start over. After the bar—Amsterdam's, where
they didn't give us a table although the place was empty so we
sat at the bar and the bartender was a big dope (by the way,
McFeely's of the urinals "like Roman steles," big as showers,
closed down: I'd heard about them and the first time I went
there for dinner I couldn't wait to take a leak just so I could
marvel at them, and when I finally had to, I walked up to one
and I don't think I should have said to the guy next to me, wow,
look how big this is) —after the bar we walked down lower
Broadway and since it was late and even though it was the
night of the St. Patrick's Day Parade no one was out and I was
looking at the cast-iron facades of buildings on the other side of
the block which were comforting and implacable, sorrowful and
witty all at the same time. This is where I used to walk late at
night when I lived in the city and didn't have anything to do
which was most of the time although you don't think of not
having anything to do in New York: there must be openings and
ballet and theater and bars, all of which is true. Most of my
friends didn't go anywhere either yet we acted like veterans of
everything. I never feel scared walking in the city and usually
when I get in this mood I materialize all over the place starting

uptown where a lot of people are walking, then head out toward
the periphery, downtown, perhaps over to Sheepshead Bay
where when I was a kid I used to dive for coins after the fishing
boats left their slips and people would stand on the bulkheads
and throw nickels or quarters (dimes were too thin) not too far
away from us but enough to make us work and to give them a
good show. My head was just above the surface and I was
shouting *over here* but when the coin entered the water and
started to drift down with this sideways scallop motion you'd
dive under and it was incredibly silent. I wore black cutoff
Levis and was very freckled. The only thing left to see by the
time I go here in one of these moods either alone or I hope with
my friends some night this spring is the Atlantic Ocean and
wherever you've arrived by then: my father who trained fighters
giving me a pair of professional boxing gloves and how every fall
we took them out of the hat box and he'd teach me how to jab.
They were an eggplant color with long ivory laces and he would
chant *left, left, right* and he came to me in a dream the other
night. A lot of us think about it, the cast-iron facades of
buildings on lower Broadway seem to say. The willing
suspension of disbelief opens into what organizes life: Boris
Karloff as The Mummy who loved his priestess through the ages
and didn't know that it wasn't the priestess who gave him his
agitated life-in-death but his own death-in-life focused on what
he loved and wouldn't give up no matter what. We're hardwired
to calibrate substance, but it doesn't measure that way until a
lot is taken from you to let you see not exactly what was "behind
it" but what emptied of number it was about. And what was it
about, that it took every day and every night from you, that of
one whom you loved nothing of worth would remain, nothing
that, knowing him or her, could make you feel what it was like
to be rushing crosstown to be there, just as when rushing
crosstown to be there, it already seemed unreal and impossible,
except for the fact—and remember that, the fact—that there
they were, not as later you would think about it, but as it was?

There's this momentum we follow toward what is not in the
world and there's no turning back, counting one after the other,
translating effects into causes, translating not ignorance but
expectation into understanding, regret, exhilaration.

Tripoline

The ultimate opera begins with an overture to Paris and Detroit. The music of this overture is two characters (one called "Paris," the other "Detroit") talking about these two capitals representing the poles between which all life occurs. Paris and Detroit have this conversation on a desert island surrounded by the bluest of blue water, a palm tree between them, and in the distance, faint smoke from a steamship that will soon rescue them. Paris mistakenly pronounces Detroit's name "daytwa." Paris is dressed in a velvet painter's smock, the kind they don't make anymore judging from the painters I know; he also wears a beret. Detroit, in honor of that city's past, is played by a full-sized car, or if that is not possible, by a glove compartment, or merely a glove. Act One is a single aria sung offstage by the heroine. She sings about her life, which doesn't seem all that marvelous or different, but it does make her sing. There's the slightest hint that if she doesn't sing the ordinariness will turn sour, though now it is not. The aria is written in Italian and Irish. It is called simply "Aria" or, in Irish, *Aria*. The classical unities are given a nod now and then, but this one-acter is more like a kiss.

Theory of Transportation

The ones we like stay later than the rest. The snow has already
changed from early evening airmail envelope blue to crisp
business letter white. In contrast, the sky is the kind of black
before night goes brilliant again with reflected light from
apartments and street lamps, constellations, the moon and other
planets you could identify. This is the first part of night
sprouting with haphazardly grouped numerals raised to this or
that power: a line of trees or an arm raised in some gesture.
Like trying to answer all the questions at the end of a chapter
in a textbook: wasn't it just a while ago we were reading the
preface with so much understanding? How did these things
come to stand for so much? It isn't as if we were in the front
row of an amphitheater looking back on other rows of seats with
numbers painted on them. That would be easy. Or even those
constellations, once you get the hang of finding them: trunk of a
horse (Pegasus) or the Big W (Cassiopeia)—a knack, like making
snowballs, and immensely satisfying, as if nature were
redeemable because constant, aloof, yet right there to squish
between your fingers if you want to get close to it, if you think
that might help. A line of trees or an arm raised in a gesture:
pine trees stoop lightly in the wind, the arm curves up and out.
You might think about what stance to take at such a moment.
Perhaps the radiance of your room, lit with such simple truths
as table and chairs, key-rings and painted wood can help.
Testimony of friends and those who love you—won't that count?
Won't that let them know what you were really up to?
Happiness, I can assure you, is this: to be let off the hook a
couple of times. It shows you how to treat others, a nonchalance
that mounts to a delectable but nonetheless rigorous morality:

your father who loved to fish but always threw his catch back in.
Too bad he didn't treat his family with the same detached
amusement. Either you wander around looking for something
larger-than-life to be your life, or you marvel at waistcoats and
thick brocade for their splendor and mystery. No, I'm not
pretending there aren't important issues to discuss, crucial
philosophical movements that arrange our minds for the
moment the way a snowstorm arranges a city. Nor do I want to
suggest that we can pretend to be "above the fray"—the hook I
want to let you off of is made of steel: it has barbs to stick in the
soft lining of your throat and not let go. Some don't get off—the
clarity of our positions is too apparent, the trajectory based on
the ground we've already covered too predictable even if the
numbers are astronomical and we can't count that high.
Somebody, or something else, can; somebody or something else is
those numbers and we are too, but their telling hangs thick as
knotted rope, thick as Welsh coal-mining songs. What would
you do? What would you like to do? These questions get
answered and an atmosphere condenses out of them, brilliant
where you want it to be brilliant, dark chocolate where that
makes sense, the raspberry lining of a jacket always a surprise.
Even in this atmosphere, where love can sort it all out, the
narrative is unflinching, grinding particulars into a kind of
paste. An arm is not a good model for a tree.

       I was saying it was getting dark out. People are starting
to come home from work and lights go on in apartments up and
down the block. Can I give you this? Can I say people are
coming home from work and lights are going on in apartments
up and down the block? No one can do that. I cannot keep you
from disappearing again. I cannot say each light places its
asterisk in the window to plead a special case, some exception.

Somebody's Terrace on Ninth Avenue

There isn't much to say about a terrace on Ninth Avenue,
or something else about your leaving the city,
or the city itself which is tiresome
although I'd like to hold on to some of the things about
that night—margaritas at the Mexican place
and how good one tasted without time for another,
the color of sky around eight o'clock,
the feel of Ninth Avenue empty that way,
and looking at the terrace sandwiched-in between the
guy taking a shower and the woman in her underwear.
Someone probably says something like this all the time.
Still, they form a part of what I have always wanted
and I love this as much as the piece of broken
planking I look at when I go down the back steps in
East Topsham, VT where a pile of cut
birch and maple lies uncovered except
first, by leaves, then snow.
I'll stack this wood so the wind can dry it out,
or buy one of those chicory-blue tarpaulins
I see other people using. This will
be our first full summer in Vermont,
lost in my love of it all winter enough to buy
an old pickup, also a weedy blue, and a yellow
plow.

     Some things speak for themselves,
some as part of others. What was it, 1,
2 in the morning when we decided to walk back to where
you live, where you once helped me find a place

—and I was lost in my love of it then too—
and the streets really did look like blacktop,
and it must've been raining while we were at John's?

Dunquin

I am walking with you on the west coast of Ireland where
Irish is still spoken. This is almost a dead metaphor,
which is why we went there. It is ten years ago
and I would rather sit in this room for an hour doing nothing
than remember walking in a dead metaphor with
hiking boots on because we thought of climbing
MacGillicuddy's Reeks but only climbed Mt. Brandon,
a talus slope, and a trail that goes through farms
where the faithful crawl on their knees on the saint's day.
Experiences take up more room than they deserve in memory
and usually don't have a point, being the
first, it looked like, to fix spaghetti for that jerk son of the
folklorist who didn't know who was buried
in the local cemetery (I was surprised, too)
and was probably cheating on his wife who asked
"Are you a morning or night person?" and I thought
she meant do I stay up late. What is an "almost
perfect" evening? Why not a perfect evening since
I'm still thinking of it, light almost to closing time at the pub
so that when it's finally dark you know you'll
have to stand up and sing the national anthem
and get chased out, a definite closing time so that
the night has at least this one limit which you get used
to and like for what it says about things. Time to
go, and some cars sputtering through first then second
gear, no street lights, no real street, brushing
against hedgerows because the road is like that
and the drink of course, and it was like a whisper getting
louder when the branches hit the side of the car.

Powder River

I want to put your postcard
into everything I do until
I finally get tired of
thinking about it.
It's on my desk between
the rock that looks like a
whale opening its mouth (three
years) and the bowl Caitie
made for me (four years).
In the bowl are my favorite pens
(Uniball blue, one year: before this
Bic Stic, half a year).
I also have the nighttime
photograph of Central Park West
(five years), a box of floppy
disks (since May, two months)
and "Landing Sardines at Low Tide"
(1880).

"I love traveling: so
many breathtaking sights and
daytrips that turn into flops."
I like that "breathtaking" which is
too trite not to mean anything:
there's nothing to prove and
you write all over the card,
over the four languages of the
name of the place they expect to
get tourists speaking in, the line

down the middle that never
gives you enough room to say
much, even the box where the
stamp's supposed to go (and
ours are so plain and theirs
sky-blue and red fading to
pink then charcoal-gray although
this one I don't get: a
woman's figure, no face, leaning
against two columns of undetermined
order since their capitals
are missing)— "Back to Italy
tonight (Naples) and then to
the French Rivera"
(Riviera). How many times
do you get to say that in one
life unless you live there and
it's like taking Amtrak from New
York to Boston if everything
was like something else which
it is not. I personally would
forget the Riviera part
but it isn't my postcard (neither
is this) and I want to hear
your "stories when we return"
more than I want to tell you
one of mine. For a drink of
water I put my hand under the
iron spigot like everyone else
in the cocktail-colored light
(Rob Roy fading to a Manhattan
with a cherry) outside a small
village in the Compero section
of Spain. I'm making it
up: I've never heard of the

Compero in Spain. But it sounds
like it could be there and
that there could be an iron
water spout and a fountain
with people standing in line for
a drink of cold water: two
Spanish policia in those plastic-
colored hats leaning against a
fig tree or stone fence.
I did once reach my hand under
this iron spigot but
not in Spain in Italy I think,
not the actual
detail that I did and where or
who with, not even the taste
or that I remember is important
as was the dull chance sweet as
clover to a cow once not missed
and forever (at least as far as
I go) not really forgotten, not
even just "misplaced" but a river
of powder of such events and the
happiness or the opposite they
rather than us are the parts of
which I seem not unpleasantly
to be supported by sometimes.

Haying

I am thinking of The Hat because I went there with you.
I am thinking of its plastic tablecloths:
I am thinking of its shrimp in hot-sauce and its real
name, El Sombrero, "The Hat" printed carefully below it
as if we'd never have figured it out for ourselves.
Who owns what, says moss on the roof.
The farmer I have to call each year to remind him I
haven't changed the terms and he can still go haying
in my fields without a fee must think it's a good
deal or he wouldn't wait for me to call, he'd
just do it. And then he cuts everything, even the
tall grass between the two tire-tracks on the skidder road.
It takes him a week to cut it and bale it and haul it away
and I've been there on weekends when the machines
he uses sit at the far end of the field
and I think, here was some big lesson about
haystacks and pitchforks I missed. All around
there are signs, some even have translations.
The waitress apologized in a blend of Spanish and English for
adding tax on the check but the city had found out about
the place and she didn't want to get into any trouble.
How can we miss it? By the end of June
the field is so deep I get halfway
to the point I like to look out from
before I have to turn around, a little disappointed, a little
   unsure.

Screenbolical

November opens a book placed on your knees
The shadow part connects letters in shade
All that we knew was right, only the corrections
Were learned or given or withheld
From children's letters

Even a sense of it was enough
The character of dimension and escape,
Who brought less to the table in the kitchen
When the floors and the windows and the chairs
Loss is not enough

Over a day or a year you might desire mixed
Grace. You might want to begin to talk about that
Like everyone else, grandeur attracts you
Although not the spectacle of their
Mouths hanging open

Gallant the knife and the fork, brilliant
The fish the knife and fork cut into, tearing
Away a bit of the meat. We used to bring
Half a lemon to school to clean ink
Off our desks

November closes early for the holidays
Reinforcing links to a past not necessarily
One's own, but then, what is, when you
Think about it, when it
Comes right down to it

So all these cleaners have lemon scent
But it wasn't the smell that was
Important, there was a chemical
Bleaching names carved into the
Wood with our

Ballpoint pens, juice running down
The desk and getting on your pants
Leaving the wood missing in the shape
Of a name. We all waited for
This day because

We didn't have schoolwork and later
We threw lemons out the window:
The old guy never thought he'd
Be in a school building again in
His life, but

He put two and two together
When a lemon hit him in the head.
Loss is not enough, the biography
Of John James Audubon will have
Birds in it

Like the sky. So he
Complained to the principal, he said
Someone hit me in the head with a lemon
And here it is! holding out
His hand, birds

Fly away from John James Audubon
Here it is, is this what you
Teach in school today, I could
Have an eye knocked out, so we
Stayed after school

All the classes on that
side of the building. No one
admitted throwing a lemon. Loss
Is not enough when we have so much
To go out to

"Lisa, Your Beautiful Friend Is Here"

she said without irony or jealousy, as if
it simply was true, as one might say your
tall friend is here, a fact everyone could see
for themselves. So it meant some things are beautiful
which never can be asserted just the right way to sound
        convincing
besides, everyone's got their own ideas and, perhaps more
        darkly,
that if something is unarguably
beautiful only some of us share in it ("your friend").
It was the way two young girls can talk about
another young girl they know, and this should get logged
        somewhere
because it's probably one of those eternal truths we
keep tripping over without knowing why: it doesn't
always get through that we were about the things that we
were doing and not that they were about us. Lisa, your
beautiful friend is here she said calmly over her shoulder
as she walked away, and "Lisa" came running out
and kissed her and hugged her as if she hadn't
seen her for a long time. Her friend, the beautiful one,
didn't know what hit her (literally, she was almost knocked
        down)
just because you can't really make someone feel everything
although you think about them all the time. "Is here" she said,
delivered finally out of whatever everything is stored in
when you can't get a look at it, and you know it's in there
even though you've never seen its face or even thought of it.

Secret Tapes

You just know how they will be able to
show us it was serially encoded, conforming
to a "current" of events like the Gulf Stream,
in effect warming us to a love for the just city
meanwhile overlooking others in a fate which is
cold and crushing and as surprisingly unsurprising
as the tide of shoppers in the checkout aisle where
everyone looks pursued by some Fury or other,
stony-faced, like high school geography teachers.
Ignorance is our own and others' problem,
and the truth is much truer, really, but I
don't want to go into that now unless you want
me to because the tokens of recognition by which
we will learn from each other are as mysteriously
funny as European telephone numbers
or an address in Queens.

                I can say a true thing
like a false one, and a false one like it
was the truth, but also a true thing like the truth.
The gates to the Academy of the Future of the Just City
have already been closed behind us, gliding effortlessly
on their hinges of ice and falling snow, with bars like
sluices for the present to keep slopping in on us,
a memory of what else is endured alone.

Looking for Halley's Comet with Liz

I still call it Hailey's
and I wanted to see a *comet*,
the kind you come to expect from
the significance everyone attaches
to their appearances and from some
sense of how things ought to look
when they are important. How
things ought to look when they
are important isn't clear but
I'd want it pretty close to the
drawings in some of the books I
had as a child which held events
and facts in tension with their meaning—
their "meaning" not the truth, but a surprise:
sparks flying out of a long silver
tail which curved up out at you, stars
and crescent moons tumbled up in it
and some glitter falling on the roofs
of the tallest buildings that now
seem refreshed not in danger of
burning up—certainly not
a dim point of light you're supposed
to look with binoculars on the
horizon for because the city
doesn't have a horizon since that
represents potential and change
while this city floats in its own
reflected light like another planet
as if to say this is it, this is

what your potential meant—happy?
Although I was glad you could come up on
the roof with me because this kind
of thing has to be shared:
appearances count, and because
they do it was fun thinking of
somebody catching us up there,
imagining some domestic
comet blazing into sight,
the kind that really does resemble
the artist's sketch. As it turned out,
only the other Ed in our building
saw us: his face looks like what I
imagine a burned-out comet
on drugs looks like. He had been
listening to WNCN too
when it was announced—a bulletin—
the comet would be visible
in half an hour. Now that I
think of it, what were they playing
while we were up there looking for
something we couldn't find and which
we can't repeat?

       What we did see
was planes circling in slow-motion
over Queens waiting to land at
LaGuardia. The historical
present fails after three seconds
or three feet and I was annoyed
at having to concentrate on
the sky when what I really wanted
to do was look at the city
all lit up. The Lower East Side
has a good view with the World Trade

Towers and the Empire State Building,
the Chrysler Building, Con Ed,
and the Waldorf floating on
top of all the other lights where
people live. I never get
tired of this sight because it
reminds me of the rides I would
take into the city with my parents
on Saturday night, and the big
feature of the trip was driving
along the Bowery to look at the bums.
I felt that this was really "life"
and what went on in flophouses
(all labeled "A Lyons House")
must be wedded to truth. I'm sure
this is why I live only a block east
of there now. Sure, "the bunkers *Born*
and *Died*" group us finally, but so what?,
returned and *left* do it in the
meantime, a series which is infinite
because you can always add on
one more episode, which means
the individual item is important—
it's already been added on
and predictability has nothing
more to do with it except as
the tail of ice and dust it comes
swinging into view with; the branching
way has been reached, all the tragedies
have found a place to park, and we
live accordingly: the fixed locale
and building height our book of hours
against a backdrop of dimly
perceived histories and astronomies,
and from here to there and back again
there are these landmarks we learn.

The Leaves Are Something This Year

1.

It makes you think when you see it spread at your feet like a
magic carpet. If I could speak the language of things, in every
description I would be asking, do you have this? Or, can I give
you this? It would say how much I loved you. It would be a
charm to protect you. And since it is a small thing, it will go
unnoticed, you will go unnoticed, although I could look now and
then and see what I guess we knew all along, expecting our
knowledge or expectations would add up to something, wouldn't
only be added on to fall off just because they do that.

2.

Shadowing this is a second set of books where the real accounts
are kept: an invisible arithmetic in long rows, some numbers so
thick they look like squirrels running up trunks of trees with
horse chestnuts in their mouths. They know. They know
ordinary methods are best, hammered out of the giant age, the
age of giants, which came after the age of smaller things, and
before this one, which is called the age of squirrels who know
best. Children and methods are buried in the ground. Do you
want to say *so much?* Do you want to say *so much* as if it were
your fate, one hand raised to the forehead, brushing back a wave
of hair?

3.

Sometimes I think I can keep myself away from you and that it
will be less trouble. Or even if I'm there, just not want you so

much, in the way of not getting too attached because it's
ultimately less painful, because there's no clarity of perception
to cut through the invisible braid of desire. You turn your hand
over and I kiss your shining wrist, exempt from everything that
does not have this mark. And I claim this. Tomorrow, last year,
have this geography. What can I give you?

4.

You are supposed to be going somewhere, in the sense of
developing and incorporating the different things that happen
into who you are, deriving yourself like an equation, factoring in
the x's and y's, where x equals any discontinuous fragment of
memory so strong it makes you feel you're still there trying to
figure out what it was for, and y, that you are the one thing that
will not translate into the purposely obscure text invented for it.
Good, let it be like that, in the sense that what continued was
the continuing part, and these other events, some of the people
or things you keep thinking about, that just seem to have
stopped, you don't get to revisit, and they don't exactly come
back, but something in-between seems to be operating, where
you don't make sense of it, with the feeling there are
underground labyrinths and life on other planets. The leaves
are really something this year: Vermonters where I go say they
haven't seen color like this for a long time. In Corbett's top floor
study there's a small volume of poems I wrote. Each time you
think the clarity will come through and part of the secret will be
eaten like cake. Each time you think this definitely has
something to do with it.

5.

Here are these big things, like fate and attraction, looking the

way they do, holding our lives to a standard of anguish and loss
and elation. I don't think there's any escape from all of this:
subtracting and subtracting until the only thing you see is what
you were going to see. The interim could make you go the stoic
route, a kind of balancing act of one absence (pain) over another
(happiness), but I don't get that, even with my lifelong
predisposition to the classics. Basically, I don't think we are
classic: we want a real test with right and wrong answers when
we step up to the examining table and have our lute and
fireman's hat taken away. I want a philosophy that is pure
description, weaving the fabric into just the way it looks. A
disappearing act, the closer I get to it, and the coin shooting
straight up my sleeve.

6.

My friend said she didn't think women fear contingency as much
as just items in a series, a continual inventory that didn't go
anywhere. To which I said some men don't say anything,
bringing an absence in the hope that a woman will fill in the
blanks, give them a kind of self-knowledge by default as if they
had to be forced into recognizing what they were doing by
having this audience to do it in front of. Not that I don't think
public gestures count, or that, say, the death of the age of
monumentality is necessarily a good thing. I can still imagine
sculpture as a noble art—the age of irony won't work in a
journal of the plague years—the unyielding made plastic and
expressive, bronze apples rolling out in front of you, looking like
they could still be soft at the center, like a sicko could hide razor
blades inside them on Halloween. We live with these things.
We live with our understanding of these things, like a character
to whom the wizard says *This is a magic torch*, and the next day
another wizard says *This is a magic torch as well.*

Still Life with Roadmap

Autumn has a way of turning into it.
Or we are always turning into autumn.
Either way it isn't too clear for too long.

First, you have the city, then upstate,
then the schools and information,
    then Maine.
Then you cross the border
and it goes: country, city, schools
    in reverse.

A horse is not a galleon. A "progress"
is a series in affirmation. First,
    you have the present tier,
    then a second.

If I have a beverage hidden in my neck
    and a cliff hidden in my neck,
who am I?
    I have a hand reaching inside my hand.

For we were always standing on a cliff
looking over at each other on a cliff,
staring at each other in the horse light—
a sheer cliff resembling the head of a horse.
I loved it the way you could turn everything into snow for
    miles around.
Night rested on our backs like a delta then:
    we were a gulf.

And I am eagerly looking forward to your return soon,
and to your wonderful small mouth on my eyes,
my eyes which are hidden in a lockpiece,
my arms in a tool and a replica.

Essays for the Moment

for Pierre Martory

1.

How they presented themselves, with such airs! You don't know
anything if you don't know me, each of them seemed to say. So
the bronze ladder, rungs burnished a pale beer color where other
hands and feet had climbed, was put aside. No, you would
never forget what was important, falling asleep on the dunce's
stool, awakening to moonlight tracing chalk on the floor of the
abandoned schoolroom.

2.

The equation may be a lot simpler than I thought. We'll let
object stand for everything you can have temporarily (length of
time not defined). "Person," therefore, is an object although we
realize this term represents more than objects, but is an object
too. For the moment we leave out everything else. *Waitress!* I
know it's their job, but on a good night you'd think the
restaurant staff had been invited and were happy to be there.
The taxi ride later is a dream, too: no bullet-proof divider, so the
driver can hear everything you're saying and—not in a pushy
way—responds with something funny and you all laugh as the
car next to you at the light looks in, the way you do at people in
cabs.

3.

If I think of a child's beach pail (a blue one, with a frieze of red

anchors around the middle) and fill it with sand and throw it in
the ocean, it makes a satisfying p-l-lop sound as water shoots up
around it like a cylinder. If I think of this pail, only empty it,
then it makes a disappointing flat sound when it hits the sea,
and floats on its side like a sailboat—given its size, a fairy-tale
sailboat, the kind a mouse and a grasshopper would go away in.
Gradually this image fades as the pail fills up with water and
then drifts with either the narrow, bottom end just touching the
surface, or the mouth end up, with the handle (a red one) folded
over to one side. Piece of junk everyone thinks who sees it
floating near them because there are certain things you don't
want to be reminded of when you go to the beach: as the day
wears on our merriment becomes more serious than this pail's
crude essay on the color of the ocean (an impossible blue), or
this joke of a frieze, a child's mythology of friendly anchors
floating through a series of repeated destinations. Piece of junk,
just like in the drugstore where you buy these beach-pail sets,
where all kinds of things are available without blending into a
definable presence: hair-dyes, ice-cream sandwiches, and
take-home tests; the pharmacist neither a doctor nor a
salesman, a special class for which only the French have
complete understanding.

4.

Yet, at least against this pale cheek, O metal god, thy titanium
hands do not always brush soft. Like any couple, we've got to
work something out. You don't want to see someone in despair,
do you? Then what about getting away for a while? But we
don't travel far before communication breaks down again, and
each day's dawning is just some better technology for carrying
your voice from even farther away. Nights are worse than the
boxes new CD's come in: you need the Jaws-of-Life to open them
too.

5.

You visit the colonial inn of your birthday and all the
"atmosphere" vanishes: the smoky mirrors, the pleasant crush at
the tavern's bar, platters of meat set out before the roisterers.
The only one standing there out of costume is you, as you begin
to attract attention and try to slow this process down because
once the tavern's customers turn to look at you, they
mysteriously disappear, leaving you standing in a re-creation of
the same exact scene, only it's in a mall, a place you never
wanted to go to, but now that you've been there a couple of
times you're used to it—besides it's the kind of place you think
you can stop going to without missing anything. "Spats" it's
called and there's a fake musket hanging on one wall and huge
copper pots on another. Some of the businessmen drink vodka
gimlets, some are having Dewars on the rocks. The bartender
feeds you a line then retreats into the darkness as if you were
about to embark upon a set speech that has become famous and
studied in all the schools because it is one of those statements of
a grand theme that we will explore in the next few weeks and I
don't think we will get any answers but we can ask a few
questions that will make us think, and this is material you will
have to know for the exam anyway. It's your birthday, so
enjoy—only it's really the myth of Narcissus you are entering, a
metamorphosis which is not the final one, only the next in a
series of continually evolving scene changes mounted like a
dream. The barroom goes dark; the actor is frozen, facing the
audience. A single spot picks him out. He speaks: "I see that
my real business is elsewhere, right here beside me, and that I
have been carrying around this weight of grief and joy like two
gym bags with their shoulder straps dragging along the ground.
I feel like I still have them, but with a good shrug I can balance
them, so that I'm standing here with a firm grip on the handles,
and there is this pleasant sensation of my arms being pulled
straight down my sides. I know it'll change soon as I start

walking—I'll have to move, you can't stand still in the middle
of such a busy street without attracting attention—but this
moment of reflection is enough to get me through the
thoughtless, chafing hours I wear like a suit of toxic side-effects.
I don't mind. But why the oppression of certain visitations, so
that the whole day is like this: a sense of loss but without
regret, just a question about what it means now that I'm feeling
it—a presence, like the gun-metal disc of a storm moving up the
coast, still many miles out to sea, coiled like an eye that is about
to look at something, not just reflect the mantle of fallen leaves?
I've got it and I want to keep it, so here, take it. It'll go anyway,
and if I don't try to hold on to anything, I won't spoil it for the
next time."

6.

Then all these periods held domain and, like disco, were
swallowed in turn by the earth which had given them life. Even
the house was infested and burned, shrieking, to the ground.
Tender love, sings the serial killer during recreation-time at the
state hospital, tender love is the glue that holds it all together,
someone's favorite dog racing across the lawn, right into the
horn-of-plenty's maw. So marks on the chalkboard began to
crystallize on the floor of the ice arena. What will take
contagion from our time? But there will always be queer,
Scottish things (for example) that fascinate us with a sense of
urgency. We know, and in this knowledge cannot keep the facts
straight very long, which allows the *Niña*, the *Pinta*, and the
Santa Maria to slip through the maelstrom like upside-down
hats pulled across on wires, pronouncing clarity on all who live
here. There will come a time—but that isn't something we
should talk about since everything will be different then.
Something immortal is a good way to preserve your impressions
and desires, and everyone you love, to keep them out of harm's

way, yet with the know-how and wherewithal to let them adapt
to new things, so some kid doesn't shout *hey Methuselah, nice
donkey-cart* when you drive up to the front of your house. No
one expected it to last very long, but we're paying for it into the
next century, now not too far away, coming towards us with its
bagpipes and its kilt.

Derivation of Equations

for Michael and Barbieo Gizzi

1.

Exact measure is the angel who departs. Fuel-spills leaching through layers of soil into the water table trace the downward stroke of her magnificent wing. Her ascension is "slow" in our language, but in her terms she is rocketing upward since she alone remarks true distance between things. 9 and 7, 2 and 5 are parts of the ever-changing format that pleased her. No derivation of equations, no tables of data twitching under countless additions and subtractions, failed to reflect the absence to which we were accustomed. It became impossible not to look.

2.

Under the weight of her look, no one gazed at the spectacular landscape without turning away sooner than later. What were you going to see? What could you see, saying to yourself "I'd really like to live here, but departure gives a kind of meaning to my life. It's what I'm accustomed to. A kind of stealth-wing apparatus I wish would go away for a while. I'd like to get to know her, take a little time to figure out some of these things on my mind."

3.

"Anything you understand is fatal." Well, maybe: I certainly

trust the person who said this, but I don't like the look of that
word "fatal." I think what she was trying to say was that quote
life was pushing her into this new place, and painful as it was
there's this crazy kind of freedom as you approach mystery or
ignorance or whatever the packing material is everything comes
in: the part's busted when you get it, and you're just winging it
anyway. That getting accustomed to this is not inferior to
understanding it.

4.

But there is no getting accustomed to it, really. Who would not
say as they poured from one hand into the other the invisible
stream of things they had known, that surely this was part of
her raiment? That in these we saw a shadow cast from her
wing. That with our first look we knew we'd never want to
depart, never want to be separated from her.

5.

Her apparent lack of motion foregrounds two aspects of desire.
First, the accustomed sense that it is a screen upon which is
cast some outline of your fate although it is not clear whether
this screen is opaque or translucent; that is, whether the shadow
is cast from in front of the screen or from behind it. If from in
front, then you have a chance of knowing more than the outline
(but what if it's you who casts the shadow?); if from behind, then
you depart with a description. Things like this we can never
know for sure. And sometimes you look at someone you love
and you think you might know. Second, who's that waiting in
the wings?

6.

Everyone—please—remain calm: take off your wings, walk
slowly out the window, down the fire escape, and across the
street. Anyway, no one is going to see her. If you could get a
look, what good would that do? Maybe it's too bad we get
accustomed to expecting more. We certainly do deserve
something more. But her departure

7.

is on privately chartered wings; no stops through Customs for
her: nothing to declare but good looks, plenty of options in the
where-to-now department.

Canvas

The don't ask part turning into the didn't need to ask you that
one part, becoming the really billowy I don't know part, later on
in summer when it's easy being casual about constants in our
lives because summer is one of them. Fatal constants perhaps,
which take into account our little deaths from our little
beginnings, meanwhile owing us everything in between. And we
like it this way and make it ours because if fate is impersonal
it's kind too, although your face is streaked with tears and the
tulip's transparent stain sets a limit to understanding. You're
always guessing what I'm thinking just when I'm about to say it,
which I like because I think that means something radiant.
Like a river flooding the low-lying towns, immortal coincidents
drown out unimmortal ones. Citizens and citizens' pets wait
patiently for rescue crews outfitted in fire-fighting gear to save
them from the roofs of their floating cars: dressing for one
natural disaster is rather like dressing for another, a call for a
perception of time unaccountably accelerated beyond the supple
bounds we placed it in even if we know a land-deal shouldn't be
too good to begin with. We learn these things. The ketchup's
red, the mustard's tulipy yellow streak by us, reappearing as
colors on a map showing borders of Hungary and Peru. The
important desires are forlornly crazy, contained within the crook
of the same tanned and tear-stained arm we shade our eyes with
on summer days when the savor of burgers and fries drifting up
through the trees projects our name on a number as clean as
salt. I can't think what it would be like to be without you,
except the charge rediscovering the whole world. Lost in each
other, we don't notice some things until like this light which is
getting longer each day we see by them.

The True Story

The true story makes it abundantly clear long after those
diverting tales about the invention of cheese and silk panties, or
the humdrum life of giants in Giantville, and how the pilgrims
made their long journey to bring one surface in contact with
another surface, like two pages facing each other in a book, with
the interest more in the passage from one place to the other and
all the changes of light and suffering on the voyage, the kinds of
tunes they played on their tin whistles, what dances, the shape
of their hats and shoe buckles, just the way our own passages
from one state, say, of happiness to another, say, of "dejection:
an ode" are more interesting, more fraught with danger than
just showing up at the amphitheater. Definitions are casually
thrown in (short-sword: a sword with a short blade), or "details
on the whole are usually concrete," and facts from biology
(vulva) as well as James Clerk Maxwell's field equation dealing
with potential (the electrical kind) until the whole thing rounds
itself out into a sort of promontory or island where we stand,
very small and very distinct, staring out into all that blue,
surprised at the amount of affection we feel for it today as we
realize how good it is not to be the first ones here having to
make up words for love or songs for jumping rope because there
are prerogatives, after all, in heritage and chromosomes and
history pulsing at our feet in little blue waves by the shore. It
really is just today, like many another day in Evening Land
where the action of the story is now taking place, although
action is hardly the word for this exquisite moment since it
doesn't matter whether we get it right or wrong; in fact, we're
supposed to fail. Our pleasure is in watching them sink out
there in the oriental surf, with the "full" knowledge that our

turn may be next—although it never is our turn because when it comes, it's different. History is all around us in the shrouds of the parachute, and it's serious this business of ours, interlinearity, writing glosses on the violet-blue text of seeming. The brain turns round in its skull-pan, or the ear is trumpet for the neck. The flowers have been roaring out their names for the sky since early this morning. Each asterisk takes off like a helicopter buzzing the inhabitants of the cove down there who are waving or water-skiing behind their speedboats. What are their names for it? The textual commentator labels it a locus classicus and corrects the spelling. At least three doctors have been collecting footnotes on my own corpus in the hope of expunging errors and bringing out a corrected text. And someday they will too, but by then the barbarians will have sacked not only the provinces but also the capital, disfiguring all the statues, and the story will have passed to other hands who will carefully pack it with the two "o's": oblivion and obliquity. The surface really is a surface this time, receding just at the point where you want to enter it—the silver screen made more out of mercury I think—although people and things are always disappearing behind it, and although these wonderfully large animal eyes stare back out at you.

Live Acts

The constitution has already been signed
and all its amendments displayed for each of us to accept
at the price of being protected by them anyway.
This is New Jersey remember, and it's still winter.
Laws that state we have a natural right
to be what we have always been sound astonishingly
true like oracles, promising as gods do in oracles
one thing we think, when, really, we learn in exile

something else: "Well, at least we were able to
speak with them," I suppose they would say in Greek.
And it translates back into you, drifting through you,
a daily tide of going out for things and coming back in,
the whole astute mess stepping disabused onto the street again,
enumerated by the birds, by the constant division of loving you.

Stage Directions

1.

Or you can track the mousy brown aftereffects as twin aluminum dashes in the far wall. Near the Williamsburg Bridge an apartment building turns its face to the light. That you couldn't be sure until now and that now you are sure move off in hunter's plaid. *Mousy brown* because the face is an angel's and doesn't need anything more, though since it is an angel nothing less. The aluminum dashes follow one another in a straight line, not one on top of the other like an equals sign; they are the highest form the short story can achieve. *An angel* because the amount of time it takes to arrive equals this.

2.

A comedy always has at least one person. Sometimes it has two people. Or it can have one person and an object, but it never has just an object, or only one person without at least an object or someone else. If it has only one person then it is a tragedy although it may not start out that way. If it has only an object then it is neither comedy nor tragedy, it is sculpture. Sculpture must never be comic: even statuary that looks odd or "funny" usually shoots us back to square one. If it doesn't—the statue to Strauss in Vienna for example—generosity and affliction fail it. The tragic "may not start out that way," but if something is going to become something else isn't it always that? These are its attributes which we experience meanwhile.

3.

Fried eggs'd be nice, you said. Fried eggs on *night*, I said, that's
what God eats! But since you had said it right the first time
you didn't know what I meant either. So we just looked at each
other, crammed into one side of the booth while the other couple
decided what they wanted. And it was all so fast and so trivial
there wasn't much to say except that I had heard an order that
could only be given in heaven.

4.

Paint chipping and falling off, wrought-iron fence revealing a
reddish-brown rustproof layer, collect their dreams too because
they only got halfway and it's beginning to sink in that I'll be
lucky to get that far if distance is measured in terms of childhood
coats that were a success. Just as you may find a sock or pair of
panties on the sidewalk outside a laundromat, these leaves have
fallen. When dignity held you in its arms it whispered, You will
make the same mistakes, the same failures will be yours. But
that isn't what you heard. Now it's important to reconstruct
what you thought it said, the ratchet-voiced next, you're next,
needs an answer.

5.

It could be a catalogue of cause and effect or a transcript of
what happens before something else happens—no cause implied
therefore, or like plastic six-pack rings or a Cyclops, not enough
of one. Meanwhile, the stage directions leave no hope for a
conclusion to the absent drama: gilt plaster cornice, pigeons
landing like sheets of pressed tin; man, face beaten color of
plum, stumbles out of bar; late afternoon, blinds close slowly in
upper-storey window; your eyes, not strictly speaking ailerons
like aluminum gashes, take my breath away.

The Ocean People Live Near the Ocean

Watching Merce Cunningham, I was thinking about Sophocles.
I mean, Euripides. I usually do think about Sophocles, picturing
a nearly vertical, white road in the middle of an otherwise
ordinary landscape. In fact, there is nothing special about this
road except its verticality and whiteness: its qualities rather
than any function it performs or destination it leads to since I
imagine it merely runs into the next village where someone who
raises donkeys is looking out across a field. The locals don't
seem to take much notice of the road either: on one side two
men are conversing as they walk away, their heads bent inward
as if they were about to lean against and support each other;
while on the other side there is more activity—three scruffy
children throwing rocks at a dog that has just wandered in as
their mothers laugh out loud at some dirty remark they have
just passed among themselves. Either a vagrant or a herdsman
(why would he be in town at midday?) is approaching from the
left, a piece of straw in his hair. Maybe it's his dog. I think of
Euripides when I see people combining not exactly against their
fate, but in spite of it, or so much a part of it that it's irrelevant.
In one dance Merce is trying to get dressed while this young
dancer keeps twirling into his space, so he has to keep moving.
We can't always keep getting undressed. Speaking of the erotic,
I was also thinking about how great everyone on stage looked.
Stage? I was thinking how great everyone in the audience
looked! What is it with dancers? I remember I was about
fifteen following this dancer all the way up Broadway. There's
that almost awkward turning out of leg muscles. I couldn't
believe how beautiful, just standing there, waiting for the light

to change. Now I usually wonder what it would be like to have
one as my own. Come to think of it, I knew that dancer who
was on a farm team for one of the big companies. Wait a
minute. I was a dancer myself! What is it with memory? My
second year at Harvard. I was sure the place was a waste of
time, but I couldn't accede to this feeling, so I started studying
lots of different things as a way of forgetting. I took Kabuki
dance with a Kabuki master who had been partially paralysed
in a car accident. How could I forget that? I learned how to
open and close a fan like a member of court (no mean feat).
There's this great dance where a woman turns into a lion. I
wonder now how I looked in class, and I wonder if there was
anyone in class watching me the way you watch someone. Life's
so stupid; I was so committed to abstraction. Who wanted me
then, and how can I reach back to them now to tell them that I
wanted them too, and that it was all for them that I wanted to
know anything about the life of history and art around me—that
I had already given up on the idea of knowledge as a connected
path, stone after stone, for the more tragic one we all know and
keep secret, opening up around us like a summer evening that
goes out and out. I remember at a party that summer I was
pushed into a shower and had my clothes stolen while I was
drying off. I hunted around for something to wear (you have to
imagine the usual while this was happening) and found an old
pair of hiking shorts which I pulled on. There's a pleasant
sensation to covering yourself after nakedness. Jokes like that
pass quickly because the next thing I remember is sitting
outside on the steps talking to you and you said you waited
almost a year to introduce yourself because I seemed so severe.
It's a good feeling to be sitting outside on a summer evening
with your shoes and shirt off making friends. And there's this
feeling that's part trees and part sky when out of nowhere
someone says they love you and you were just thinking along
those lines yourself and there's the whole summer ahead of you.
It works out that way and there's so much to talk about.

Odeon

Soon as you see someone in a cab at night
you want to look at them basically because of
the drama of something shiny in the dark
like a yellow taxi, the way
skylines are very nice to look at, or of course
those more fundamental kinds of skyline,
constellations, which form an end to our
way of thinking. The city is a kind of constellation
if you want to get fancy:
picture a map of the U.S. in the dark
with the major cities against it with all
their lights on. I like that:
this is "Chicago" instead of a useless
Greek mythological reference which does
express a truth about something, but to so few.
New York. And these would be new references
which have already been well established
but which are still surprising and disgusting
as I imagine various myths must have been since they
rarely mention disease except as plague, which is a
legality. The lesson was that it was supposed to be
condign: the same yellow school bus
with one face pressed against the window
and attendance being kept—or pain is very
dark but will be light-filled, not this limestone
daylight which cuts across our hands,
but the light which both of us love
when it fails innumerably throughout the city.

Viking Melody

Mixed blessings in disguise—likeness repeats the offers:
politeness and being and the forfeit of nuance. It won't last out
the year, if even this day, which is falling into the well of noon
like a green apple.

Loss is the intuition of our giant stature. Someday you will
roar out the names of the entire stock. That moment will endure
forever.

Last night in the yoke of destiny, yoke as in the egg-kind, not
the ox-type—destiny, by the way, is more like the egg-kind than
the ox-type, which calls to mind the feeling of having to plow
the fields, probably rice paddies of some sort: although I could
accept the idea of destiny like a rice paddy being plowed, not the
plowing or having to plow it like an animal, but look how many
people live off rice because they don't have anything else to eat.

The oracular responses that have been preserved are not the
mystical statements about life you'd expect: marry this one,
plant barley not wheat, sail in August the weather is better then.
I didn't know anything until I saw the silver line along the trees
streaming into your hip.

Never misspelling a word I once said was what passion was like
if you didn't know what it meant (say you were an alien from
outer space) and you only had a limited experience of our world
and one of those experiences was having to learn our language
so that when you got here you could converse with us and ask

questions about what we know and how we lived. "Earthling, you have made us understand passion; we thank you, and we feel some sorrow now that we must destroy your planet but that is our sole mission in coming here. Do not ask why; we do not entirely understand it ourselves. But this night will show stars in heaven as you could never imagine them."

We're told so many things about happiness. In one version it's like coming upon a thick vein of nickel in a mine shaft: sure, you're rich, but everyone calls you Mr. Nickels.

How much life at this time of year! But for now the surface was not betrayed. In each were honor and misfortune. And one day she opened her hand to the weather, to the buildings on lower Broadway, to a new way of including what had happened.

Morfudd's Hair

after Dafydd ap Gwilym

Now you're famous in two towns:
the one where I used to live
and your own.
I say where I used to live because
now I live only when we meet
and your cruel gold hair
comes honey and fruit.

There's a certain tact in not always killing everyone with
        good looks
which you must find hard to appreciate.
You bring with you a slim,
cloudless feeling of sky,
the sort of ordinary, beautiful,
clear-blue day I want to climb up a rope into,
a rope of hair let down for me alone,
looking around in disbelief,
and not tied on to anything more substantial
than a wish that counts.

You will always be someone's preference,
which feeds my bad discomfort
and my good one, the one that makes me evasive
and fun to be with you: if I try to
push you away it's phony and fateful
like fate
pushing us to discover what we can't, thanks, know
because we are it.

I see a small circle of waves in your hair when I look again.

The chargedly bright dark
when we go for a walk is the city around itself.

Fragment of a Haiku

How long can that last?
The sky really clobbered us this time
You somehow learned the night before
With delight. An armature
The next day we're back on the ground
The face of a perfect statue
And stand aside for a while
Staring at the missing head
Those big summer nights that go up and up
As if summer were really like that.
The rest just seem to lead away
Blonde sheathing all around
Since it probably destroys you

The sorcerer's apprentice in his conical hat
Some ring or mark is usually found
We still admit to desire
In which other things get done and change
Experiencing knees, need-to-know
Although you are dying
Each day a new language
Going to bed with you
Others are less believed in
And the knowledge that flows from this
We understand it all fluently
Two women hold out their arms
In contrasting circumstances
Like a city in Sophocles

Though we are what we have been calling evening
Under a different name

Nine Acts That Would Have Killed Vaudeville

1.

Two men in checkered flannel shirts, stage right; center stage, bow of ocean liner under construction. Lunch whistle. Shadow of bird glides across hull.

2.

Jack, a six-foot puppet, opens apartment window and steps onto fire escape. City noises below—faint, joyous. Jack, in red plaid shirt and jeans, is a dishwasher by day. Late summer night, still hot and muggy. He leans on fire escape railing, then sits on bottom step of ladder leading to floor above. He rises, leans on fire escape again. Jack sings to the moon and the stars then retires for the evening. He sings about his job as a dishwasher, he sings about some times in the morning that he likes a lot, about late afternoon and friends he has. The moon, so taken by his song, and the Pleiades also, come down to his fire escape. The Pleiades spin rapidly around the moon (it is a crescent moon).

3.

Ink well, stage left. Stage right, nib of fountain pen enters. Sound of heavy rain.

4.

Fishermen, stern of ocean trawler. They wear bright yellow
storm-pants with yellow suspenders. Crackle of radio in back-
ground. They haul in net glistening with fish. Stage left, lights
come up to reveal a tableau vivant: *Czarina Elizaveta Petrovna
Receiving Russia from the Hands of Her Dying Father, Peter
the Great.*

5.

Forest ranger, lonely outpost of national park. Midnight.
Strange light accompanied by "other-world" sounds. Scene
changes: Longfellow House, Brattle Street, Cambridge,
Massachusetts. Main sitting room, Longfellow memorabilia
prominently displayed. Same light, sounds as before.
Memorabilia begin to shake.

6.

Tom-toms. Large coffee (really large, about seven feet high, one
of those take-out containers with generic Greek frieze running
around the sides), milk no sugar, descends center stage.
Tom-toms continue until coffee touches stage, then silence, stage
goes dark.

7.

Henry Wadsworth Longfellow, age seventeen, enters stage right,
clothes torn, face bloodied, carrying soul of defeated alien from
another world, which before it departs to its own notion of
Paradise, bestows gift of poetical powers on young Hank. He
begins reciting *Hiawatha.*

8.

Stage dark. Sound of subway train rumbling through tunnel;
comes to stop. Sound of train doors opening and closing; sound
of train departing. Light comes up to reveal Times Square
Station, 3 A.M. Groups of homeless people barely visible, asleep
in corners of station. Slowly, a man identified only as "City
Official" descends stairs, stage right, and from deep inside his
coat pulls out bucket of gold coins which he begins to pour into
sleeping man's pockets. City Official backs away and from stage
left a shaft of radiant light, parallel to plane of stage, bathes his
surprised and happy face. Shaft of light disappears causing
momentary confusion and doubt, then reappears. This action
repeats many times until City Official, perplexed, exits. Stage
cleared, light continues to shine then disappear.

9.

Henry Wadsworth Longfellow, near death, is carried aboard
waiting spaceship.

Vermont House

So this is late spring turning (very soon)
to summer,
this is Vermont in New York
at the end of the day
when the city can be anything I want it to be,

not hungry, not thirsty
not speaking a totally foreign language
as it might look
on a white page,
everybody heading home, heading out

across the rivers, the East and North,
the Harlem, which I admit I've never said,
"Well, let's go look at the Harlem River"
as I have said "Let's go look at the
Gowanus Canal" on Carroll Street in

Brooklyn, so filthy my soul
wants to swim in it, but I don't
so *we* won't. I used to swim in it
as a kid, people have told me,
and I believe them because

something can change in a short time
so that it's gone forever
and you wish it would come back.
The canal has the best view
of the city except for the

ferry's which is spectacular,
so this is the best one on land
(except for the Promenade).
But no one goes to the canal,
no one flings open a window

and shouts, "Wouldn'cha know it,
this stinking canal, but what
a view!" The Vermont house
sits on top of a hill much more
complicated than a child's drawing

of a hill which is only an extended
wave or wavy line, all up and then
down, more of an elbow point
as you might see it
breaking the water by a

swimmer. The Vermont house hill
has a much broader top (we say
"top of the hill," "hilltop," but
"has a top" sounds wrong), a field
where in winter a plane landed on

skis instead of wheels. The house
is really a cabin or "camp"
as they say in Vermont, come over
to my house, meaning apartment,
as I and my friends said

growing up in Brooklyn. Ignorance
is one of the big stories,
another is the simple
exchange of place and the loss or
finding of people you love.

It never balances out (think
what that would mean), one always
upstages the other: a chorus
from Aeschylus when you were
hoping for a laugh: or—harder

still?—when you want to slip into
something more tragic, the scene
changes (the sun comes out after
a grey morning, someone you were
dying to hear from calls) and

everything is different.
It comes down to this: saying
hello or goodbye. You hope more
one than the other—sometimes you
don't know which, it's like a splinter

in your finger. The hellos form
one team and the goodbyes are also
on that team. If you have
too much of one (hellos, for
example) you may be happy

or not choosy or desperate.
But simple addition has nothing
to do with how we feel. A cast
or spin, lines all going in one
direction, can be given to

your whole life by one departure.
Some never recover: subtraction
is not so simple. But it's
also true that one meeting,
by chance or sometimes by plan

or simply you've changed, can erase
everything and you get to start
over. Not really, the ignorance
part is also not so simple
after the first true ignorance

that makes things grow like annual
rainfall, or giant bursts
of ignorance sweetening the air
like a thunderstorm in humid
August. No, not knowing becomes

difficult to manage and is
a blossom you will not easily
get a whiff of although it is
always right there riding a car's
fender or in those white starburst

flowers we saw on the road near
the Vermont house. By mistake you
uprooted the one we took back,
surprised that it was what you thought
it was and that it grew so far north.

Toward Blue Peninsula

Well, and which fun moment did you make,
finding it torn and not that torn,
the way an open door at morning
appears with sunlight raking
through it? And it leaves no wake
although we are being drawn
to it, where everything and nothing is being born
again. And it is not opaque.

Each loss becomes a way of looking at it
as we approach that
blue peninsula I was telling you about,
the one with the white
grating peeling back from it
like a grid.
Just to be a part of you is already miles,
a landscape dreaming us into itself,
as if arriving could really be untragic
though charged by the products of its lessening.

Common Preludes

1.

I suppose it's realizing a remainder is left over and this remainder cannot be factored in.

2.

Severing stars from one another, listing wedge-shaped nights

3.

Once the position is established, near the front of the head and down the side. Like everyone else, we had a haunted house in our neighborhood.

4.
for Steve Tapscott

So I felt this lack of a higher mathematics.

5.

Notes for a translation of *The Persians*: names are recited in the dark and throughout the play. Even when an actor is delivering a line this chorus of names is heard in the

background, undramatic, on tape, like a grammar school
teacher taking attendance, as if they could answer, *here, here.*
At first the audience will have vivid yet fleeting associations
with these names but will soon grow bored, then irritated ("What
is this about? How did I get roped into coming here?") as the
recitation continues with no action. The theater itself (seats all
facing the same way, the heavy folds of curtains) stands in for
this unconventional chorus. The audience has a role to play
too, very different from the teacher dispassionately taking
attendance, the three seconds of consciousness that constitute
the historical present before the student sinks back into the
class, attention freed from waiting for a name to be called out,
classical unity of time and place. This absence, repetitious yet
changing from point to point, alternately attended to and
forgotten, this invisible chorus is the play, the play a grid
overlapping an unseen presence.

6.

for John Ashbery

When they tore down the haunted house, all us kids felt a little
off balance.

7.

I think we're imprinted on destructive forces and follow them
around as if they could tell us something about who we are or
where we come from. During the hurricane I went out for a walk
and was almost killed when the letter "K" from Key Food blew
down on top of me. Key Food was Mullen's Furniture first and
in the way I regard myself as a theorem that is proved only
from other propositions already given as true, always will be

Mullen's. Thus, knowing that mattresses were once stacked in the meat section made us shop at Bonson's Delicatessen for day-to-day things like butter and eggs; besides, Key Food didn't have the reputation of A&P next door to Live Fish with barrels of blue-claws on the sidewalk, caught locally in New York waters which hadn't yet collapsed. Life was pretty big then and a lot of what I took for granted—barrels of crabs on the sidewalk for example—was anti-mysterious: you were supposed to take it for granted, and if you had a hankering for crabs one night you went down and got a bucketful.

8.

I saw a production of *The Persians* for the first and, so far, the last time when I was a sophomore in college. The performance was in Manhattan at either the original Roundabout Theater (now an indoor tennis court) or a church (maybe still a church). I thought the play was boring: "I thought it was static," I said in reply to the question, "What did you think?" coming from the Greek teacher who brought us to the play. He taught classics to high school students and I think he asked me what I thought to show me off (a "college man") to his students. He was disappointed with my reply, as I was, because I immediately intuited that something else must have been going on there with a dead king dressed in what I now remember was a Kabuki costume walking stiffly up some stairs center stage. "Despair is static," he replied and turned to another student who was holding on to the same pole I was as the subway lurched uptown where he lived. I don't remember how I fell in with this group, but I was always "falling in" with people then, the result of a decision I had made about going to college, about not worrying what to do once I was there except to fill in what I didn't know, thinking that because I didn't know it, it must be valuable. I threw myself into Greek with the abandon of a seal playing in a bed of kelp. All the time I was looking for an answering

knowledge in the self to mature—that was what I wanted,
deeper than the time-line approach to learning, first comes this,
then that, rising like particles of light in the water table until it
became a city with truth rolling out in front of me on the
counter-top with the satisfying feel of oranges rolling out of a
paper bag.

9.

for Ann Lauterbach

You could catch blue claws on the side of the Brooklyn
waterfront that looked out to Sandy Hook. This one spot on the
dock I remember near the table with the hose where fishermen
cleaned fish by chopping off their heads and slitting them down
the belly then sticking the hose inside was a good place to catch
blue claws because they clustered on the pilings waiting for
those fish heads. I had this long pole with a string net at the
end and would reach down and scrape them off the piling which
had barnacles on it so by the end of the summer the net was
pretty frayed. You had to scrape up the piling then twist the net
over to the side you thought the crab was going to swim away in
so that it went right into the net instead, then continue
sweeping the net sideways through the water against the
direction the crab was swimming, twisting your wrists slightly
to lift the crab above the surface of the water before it could
reverse direction and get away. I practiced this a lot before I
got the hang of it but eventually it became one of those things
you know how to do so well you localize knowledge in part of
your body—"It's all in the wrists"—a knack. It's when you're
operating on this mechanical level you're "lucky" in the thing
you're doing, maybe even "happy" in a more general sense, an
unthinking cog in the machine which we usually think of as a
bad thing because it's supposed to mean you don't have any free
will or you're unimportant in contrast to the rest of it or doing
something you don't understand the reason for—all of which,

let's face it, is pretty much true in a lot of life, especially the middle of eternal August with its sleepless nights and industrial-strength cicadas making that winding noise so that you think there never can be anything else except more loss and fulfill-ment.

10.

The rest of the evening is a blur; I was too embarrassed to relax. I think of that play now without trying to think of anything I learned about it—those things are in solution anyway, leaching out like compounds forming in the soil. I sort of tunnel into the play, redesigning the interior the way some people buy into older buildings, gutting large sections of them, but carefully preserving a few original details as if they provided clues to another hidden life within this daily subtracted one that mysteriously reappears each morning, though night with its royal hand, all flourishes on the first line of vellum, grants its dispensation and orders something new in its place.

11.

for William Henry Barrett

I wanted to write a play where because of some magic I would be able to see you again. You would be standing on a busy downtown corner near the subway exit and waving to me as I crossed the street—for some reason I am a few minutes late. You wouldn't be able to leave the corner so we'd have to stay there, but we could talk and I would tell you what had been going on in my life and you would sometimes smile at what I was saying or because you were glad to see me again. We would talk about the usual things, and I would ask you for advice about some of them, which was always my way of saying what I had already decided. We might even run out of things to talk about, but we sometimes did this so it would be alright, and we would look at what was going on around us until we remembered the next thing we wanted to say. Then you would have to go and I would say I love you, and you would say I love you too Ed, and you would walk down the subway entrance and I would go home again. And maybe I could arrange it so that we did this once a year, a series of meetings with you waving and smiling at me from across the street.

12.
for William Corbett

The scoreboard is lit up as usual.